HOLIDAY ORNAMENTS
FOR THE SCROLL SAW

BY RICK AND KAREN LONGABAUGH

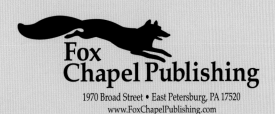

Fox
Chapel Publishing

1970 Broad Street • East Petersburg, PA 17520
www.FoxChapelPublishing.com

© 2005 by Fox Chapel Publishing Company, Inc.

Holiday Ornaments for the Scroll Saw is a compilation of projects featured in *Holiday Scrollsaw Ornaments* by Rick and Karen Longabaugh. The patterns contained herein are copyrighted by The Berry Basket. Readers may make three copies of these patterns for personal use. The patterns themselves, however, are not to be duplicated for resale or distribution under any circumstances. Any such copying is a violation of copyright law.

Bibliographical note
Holiday Ornaments for the Scroll Saw is a revised and expanded republication of *Holiday Scrollsaw Ornaments*, originally published in 1999. This edition of the work includes expanded instructions for getting started along with full-color photos and full-color photos of a selection of the finished projects.

ISBN-13: 978–1–56523–276–1
ISBN-10: 1–56523–276–3

Publisher's Cataloging-in-Publication Data

Longbaugh, Rick.

    Holiday ornaments for the scroll saw / by Rick and Karen
Longabaugh. -- East Petersburg, PA : Fox Chapel Publishing, c2005.

       p. ; cm.

       ISBN: 1-56523-276-3
       ISBN-13: 978-1-56523-276-1

       1. Christmas tree ornaments--Patterns. 2. Wood-carving.
       3. Handicraft. 4. Jig saws. I. Longabaugh, Karen. II. Title.

    TT199.7 .L66 2005
    745.594/12--dc22   0509

Printed in China
10 9 8 7 6 5 4 3 2 1

To learn more about the other great books from Fox Chapel Publishing, or to find a retailer near you, call toll-free 1-800-457-9112 or visit us at **www.FoxChapelPublishing.com**.

Note to Authors: we are always looking for talented authors to write new books in our area of woodworking, design, and related crafts. Please send a brief letter describing your idea to Peg Couch, Acquisition Editor, 1970 Broad Street, East Petersburg, PA 17520.

Alan Giagnocavo
Publisher

Peg Couch
Acquisition Editor

Gretchen Bacon
Editor

Troy Thorne
Design

Linda L. Eberly
Jon Deck
Layout

Jon Deck
Cover Design

Rick and Karen Longabaugh started The Berry Basket and Great American Scrollsaw Patterns—their family-owned online and mail order company, specializing in unique and useful scroll saw patterns and accessories—in the fall of 1990. What began as one set of collapsible basket patterns became a complete line of full-size woodworking patterns and hard-to-find accessories.

Rick has been featured on the popular PBS show *The American Woodshop* with Scott Phillips and also on the cover of *Popular Woodworking* magazine. Many of their unique projects have been published in a number of woodworking publications, including *Wood* magazine, *Creative Woodworks & Crafts*, *Popular Woodworking*, *The Art of the Scroll Saw*, *Scroll Saw Workshop*, and Patrick Spielman's *Home Workshop News*.

To find materials and supplies for scroll sawing, contact The Berry Basket, PO Box 925, Centralia, WA 98531, 1–800–206–9009, **www.berrybasket.com**.

INTRODUCTION

Holiday ornaments are among the favorite projects of scrollers worldwide. Generally cut from thin hardwoods or plywoods, ornaments are quick and easy, as well as inexpensive, to make.

This book features a variety of projects from The Berry Basket's unique ornament collection. Precise patterns and easy-to-follow instructions will enable you to complete your project with professional results, and you'll also find some basic scroll sawing tips and techniques to get you started.

We have designed these ornaments in a variety of themes, including angels, children, holiday greetings, Santas, snowflakes, snowmen, Victorian, wildlife, and more. With over 300 choices, there's sure to be something for every décor.

GETTING STARTED

The following scroll saw tips and techniques are intended to get you started and on your way to scroll saw success. You will find these techniques helpful in completing the projects in this book as well as other scroll saw projects.

SAFETY TIPS

Always keep safety in mind as you are working. Below are some general safety guidelines to take into consideration before you begin.

- Use glasses, goggles, or similar equipment to protect your eyes.
- Remove any loose clothing or jewelry before you operate your saw.
- It is always a good idea to work in a well-ventilated area. Consider using a mask, an air cleaner, a dust collector, or any combination of these to protect your lungs from fine dust.
- Be sure that your work area is well lighted.
- Keep your hands a safe distance away from the blade.
- Don't work when you are tired or unfocused.

COPYING THE PATTERN

The patterns contained in this book are intended to be your master patterns. We recommend making photocopies of the project pieces and then using a repositionable spray adhesive to adhere them to your workpiece. This method of transfer is easier, less time-consuming, and far more accurate than tracing. Using a photocopier will also allow you to enlarge or reduce the pattern to fit the size

Figure 1. Be sure to sand the workpiece before applying the pattern. You may also want to sand the wood lightly once you have cut the design and removed the pattern to eliminate any "fuzz" and to get rid of any glue residue.

of wood you choose to use. Please note that some photocopy machines may cause a slight distortion in size, so it is important to use the same photocopier for all of the pieces of your project and to photocopy your patterns in the same direction. Distortion is more likely to occur on very large patterns.

PREPARING THE SURFACE

For most projects, it is best to sand the workpiece prior to applying the paper pattern and cutting the design (see **Figure 1**). Once you've cut the design and removed the paper pattern, it may be necessary to lightly sand any glue residue remaining, along with any "fuzz" on the bottom side.

TRANSFERRING THE PATTERN

Using a repositionable spray adhesive is the easiest and quickest way to transfer a pattern to your workpiece after photocopying it. (These adhesives can be found at most arts and crafts, photography, and department stores. Pay special attention to purchase one that states "temporary bond" or "repositionable.")

Start by setting up in a well-ventilated area. Lightly spray the back side of the paper pattern, not the wood (see **Figure 2**). Allow it to dry only

Figure 2. Use "repositionable" spray adhesive to adhere your patterns to the wood. A simple glue box, made from a common cardboard box, helps to confine the adhesive.

until tacky—approximately 20 to 30 seconds. Then, apply it to the workpiece, smoothing any wrinkles if necessary.

One of the most common problems with using repositionable spray adhesive for the first time is applying the right amount onto the back of the pattern. Spraying too little may result in the pattern's lifting off the project while you are cutting. If this occurs, clear Scotch tape or 2" clear packaging tape can be used to secure the pattern back into position. Spraying too much will make it difficult to remove the pattern. If this occurs, simply use a handheld hair dryer to heat the glue, which will loosen the pattern and allow it to be easily removed.

SELECTING THE MATERIALS

Selecting the type of material that you will use is very important for the final outcome of your project. All of the projects in this book have been designed so that hardwoods, plywoods, or a combination can be used to create your work of art.

Hardwoods offer a wide variety of species, colors, and grain patterns; however, they are more time-consuming to cut, require more sanding, are more likely to warp, and are more expensive to use (see **Figure 3**). Generally, any of the domestic or imported varieties will work well—ash, maple, walnut, oak, birch, mahogany, cherry, and hickory

Figure 3. Hardwoods offer a variety of colors and grain patterns that can enhance your projects. Shown here from left to right are catalpa, red oak, cherry, birch, black walnut, white oak, mahogany, and American aromatic cedar.

Skip Tooth Blades

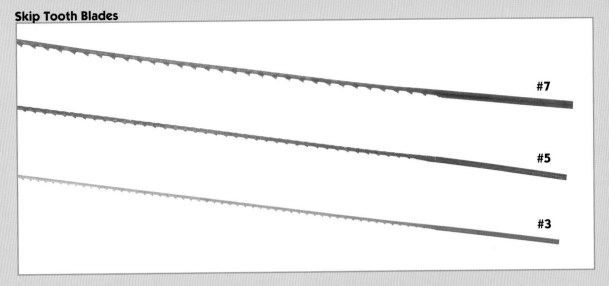

#7

#5

#3

Figure 4. Skip tooth blades can be good blades for a beginning scroller. Pictured here from bottom to top are skip tooth blades #3, #5, and #7.

are just a few of the common types.

Plywoods, on the other hand, are less expensive, require less sanding, and come in a variety of standard thicknesses. They also are less likely to develop cracks or to warp. We do, however, recommend that you use top-grade plywood without voids, such as the Baltic and Finnish birches.

Unless otherwise noted, choose stock that is ¹⁄₁₆" to ⅛" thick for the ornament projects in this book.

BLADE SELECTION

There are many opinions regarding which blade to use, depending on which type and thickness of material you choose and on how intricate the design in the project is. The more time you put into scrolling, the more your choice of which blade to use will become personal preference.

For the beginning scroller, we recommend skip tooth blades, but be sure to experiment and find the blade that suits you best (see **Figure 4**). We also offer the following blade size guidelines to get you started:

Material Thickness	Blade Size Recommended
¹⁄₁₆" to ¼"	#2/0, #2, or #3
¼" to ½"	#5 or #7
½" to ¾" or thicker	#7 or #9

SQUARING THE BLADE

Before you begin cutting, it's a good idea to check that your table is square to the blade. Lift the saw arm up to its highest point and place a 2" triangle or a small square beside the blade (see **Figure 5**). If the blade and the square aren't parallel to each other, adjust your table until both the blade and the square line up.

Figure 5. One way to check if your table is square to your blade is to use a small square. Place the square next to the blade and adjust the table as necessary until the blade and the square are parallel.

If you don't have a square or triangle, try this method using a piece of scrap wood. First, make a small cut in a piece of scrap wood (see **Figure 6**). Then, turn the scrap wood until the cut is facing the back of the blade. Slide the wood across the table so that the blade fits into the cut. If the blade inserts easily into the cut, it is square. If the blade does not insert easily into the cut, adjust the table until the blade is square.

CREATING AN AUXILIARY TABLE

Most scroll saws on the market today have an opening in the table and around the blade that is much larger than you need. This design often causes small and delicate fretwork to break off on the downward stroke of the blade. An easy solution is to add a wooden auxiliary table to the top of the metal table on your saw.

To make an auxiliary table, choose a piece of ¼" to ⅜" plywood that is similar to the size of your current saw's table. If you wish, you can cut this plywood to the same shape as the metal table on your saw, or to any shape or size you prefer. We do recommend, however, that you make the table larger than what you think you will need for the size of the projects you will make in the future.

Next, set the auxiliary table on top of the metal table. From the underside of the metal table, use a pencil to mark the location where the blade will feed through. Then, turn the auxiliary table over and drill a ¹⁄₁₆"- to ⅛"-diameter hole, or a hole slightly larger than the blade you will be using.

Finally, apply a few strips of double-sided carpet tape to the metal table on each side of the blade. Firmly press the auxiliary table onto the double-sided carpet tape, making sure that the blade is centered in the hole.

DRILLING BLADE ENTRY HOLES

If your project requires blade entry holes, be sure to drill all of them once you have adhered the paper pattern to the workpiece with repositionable spray adhesive. When drilling blade entry holes, it is best to drill close to a corner, rather than in the middle of the waste areas, because it will take less time for the blade to reach the pattern line (see **Figure 7**). Sand the back of the piece to remove any burrs before you begin cutting.

Figure 6. If you don't have a square, you can use a piece of scrap wood to square the table to the blade. First, make a small cut in the piece of scrap wood. Then, slide the cut toward the blade from the back. If the blade fits into the cut easily, the table is square to the blade.

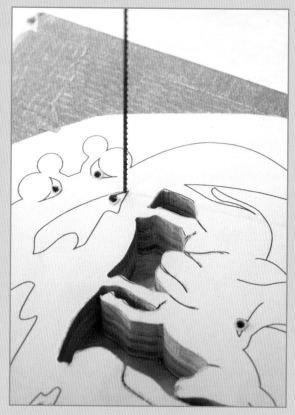

Figure 7. Drill any blade entry holes close to corners so that it will take less time for the blade to reach the pattern line.

Figure 8. Veining can give your projects a lifelike appearance. Many times veining areas will be as simple as cutting inward from the outside edge.

VEINING

Veining is a simple technique that will bring a lifelike appearance to your project. The veins of a leaf or the folds of clothing will look more realistic when this technique is incorporated.

To vein, simply choose a thin blade (usually smaller than #7) and saw all solid, black lines as indicated on the pattern. You will be able to vein some areas of the pattern by sawing inward from the outside edge (see **Figure 8**); in other areas, you will need to drill a tiny starter hole for the blade.

If you wish to make a project easier, simply omit the veining.

STACK CUTTING

Stack cutting is fairly simple to do and can save you a lot of time when you have two or more identical pieces to cut for a project or if you are making more than one of a particular project. If you are fairly new to scroll sawing and stack cutting, we recommend cutting no more than a total thickness of ½" for best results.

On projects with fairly simple shapes, two or three layers could be held together by double-sided tape or by paper sprayed on both sides with glue and sandwiched between the workpieces. You could also put masking tape on each edge of the stack to hold the pattern and the workpieces in place (see **Figure 9**).

On more intricate projects, we suggest using #18 wire nails or brads that are slightly longer than the total thickness of the stack you are cutting. Tack the nails into the waste areas you will cut out, along with a few around the outside of the project. If the nail has gone through the bottom of the workpiece, use a hammer to tap it flush or use coarse sandpaper to sand the points flush with the bottom of the workpiece.

If you are stack cutting hardwoods, do not tack the nail too close to the pattern line or it may cause the wood to split. You could also predrill holes for the nails with a slightly smaller drill bit so the nail will fit snugly and hold the layers together securely.

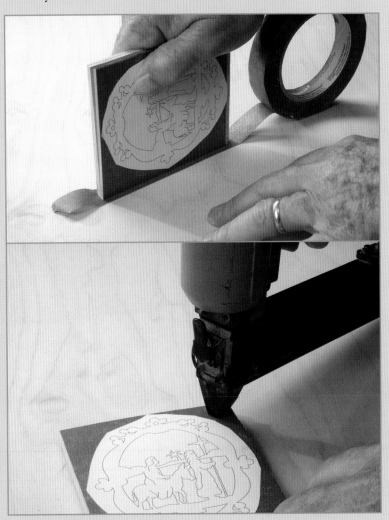

Figure 9. Masking tape or painter's tape (shown) placed around the edges can be used to hold a stack together. Some scrollers also like to cover the surface of the wood with tape before adhering the pattern to help lubricate the blade as it cuts. Driving nails in the corners of the stack can also be an effective method of holding the stack together.

SAWING THIN WOODS

Thin hardwoods or plywoods can be difficult to work with because they're prone to breaking. The following suggestions should help to eliminate or reduce this problem.

- If you have a variable speed saw, reduce the speed to ½ to ¾ of high speed.
- If you do not have a variable speed saw, it will help to stack cut two or more layers of material to prevent breakage.
- For cutting any thickness of material, it is very beneficial to keep the fingers of at least one hand, if not both, partially touching the table for better control.
- Using a smaller blade with more teeth per inch helps to slow down the speed at which the blade is cutting. However, if the blade is leaving burn marks, you will need to slow the saw speed down or use a blade with fewer teeth per inch.

FINISHING TECHNIQUES

If you've made your project from hardwood, we recommend dipping it in a dishpan or a similar container filled with a penetrating oil, such as Watco or tung (see **Figure 10**). After dipping the project, allow the excess oil to drain back into the pan, and then follow the manufacturer's instructions.

Figure 10. If you have used hardwood for your project, an easy method of finishing is to dip the project in a dishpan or a similar container filled with a penetrating oil.

If you have chosen to use plywood, such as Baltic birch, you can use any of the wide varieties of wood stains available on the market. We do, however, recommend sanding the surface thoroughly in order for the plywood to accept the stain more evenly.

As a final finish step, use a clear, Varathane-type spray for a protective coating.

HANGING THE ORNAMENTS

As you look over the patterns in this book, you will notice that some patterns do not have a circle indicating where to drill the hole for hanging. This typically indicates that the ornament is not symmetrical. To determine where to drill the hole, take a length of string or ribbon and tape it to where you think it may hang best. You can then reposition the string as needed, without leaving any marks or holes, until you find the balance point. Once you determine where to drill, remember to mark your master pattern in the book for future use.

ANGELS AND NATIVITY

Cut 2 angels

Attach to backside of the ornament on dashed line.

Dashed lines indicate placement of figures. Attach with glue or silicone.

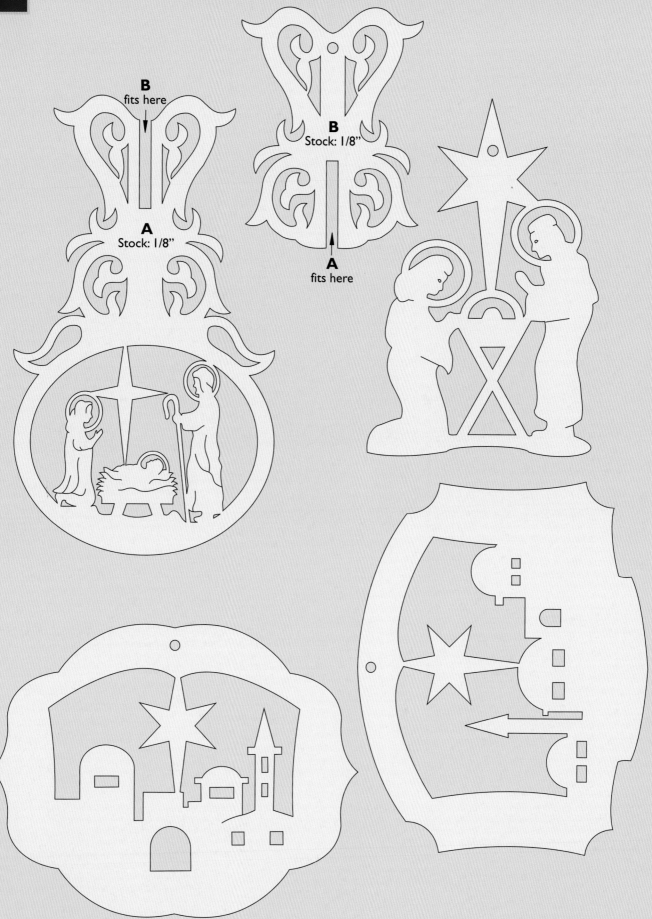

B
fits here

A
Stock: 1/8"

B
Stock: 1/8"

A
fits here

B
fits here

B
Stock:
1/8"

A
fits here

A
Stock: 1/8"

B
fits here

A
Stock: 1/8"

B
Stock: 1/8"

A
fits here

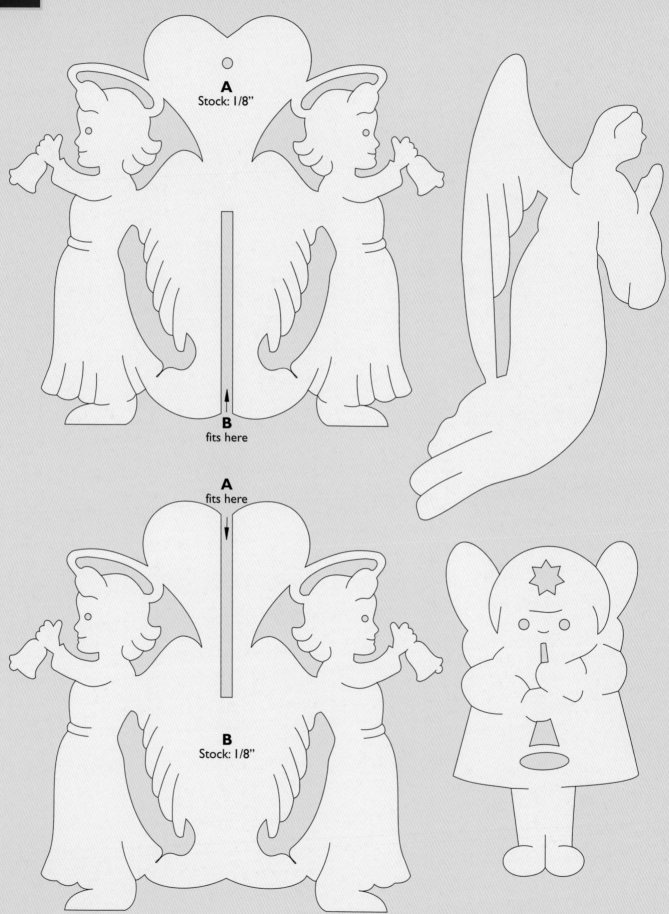

A
Stock: 1/8"

B
fits here

A
fits here

B
Stock: 1/8"

Number option.

Number option: glue the number pattern piece(s) into position on the angel and cut out. Good for birthday ornaments, etc.

Number option.

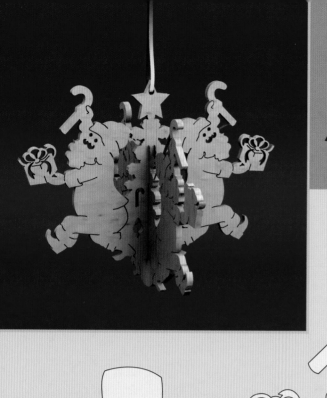

SANTAS, ELVES, AND SNOWMEN

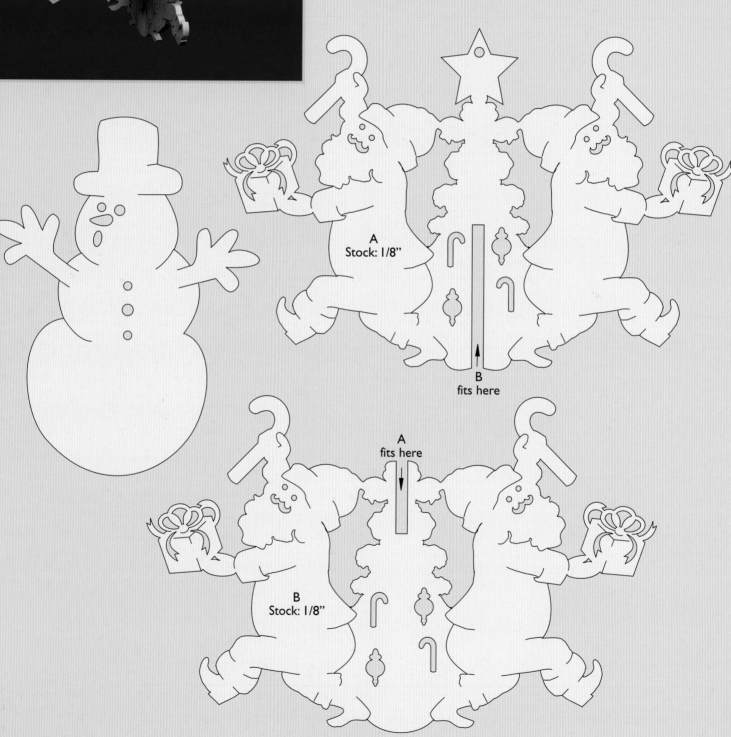

A
Stock: 1/8"

B
fits here

A
fits here

B
Stock: 1/8"

Dashed lines indicate position of overlay, secure with silicone.

A
fits here

B
Stock: 1/8"

A
Stock: 1/8"

B
fits here

Option: attach elf to tree with glue or silicone.

Dashed lines indicate position of arms on backside, secure with silicone.

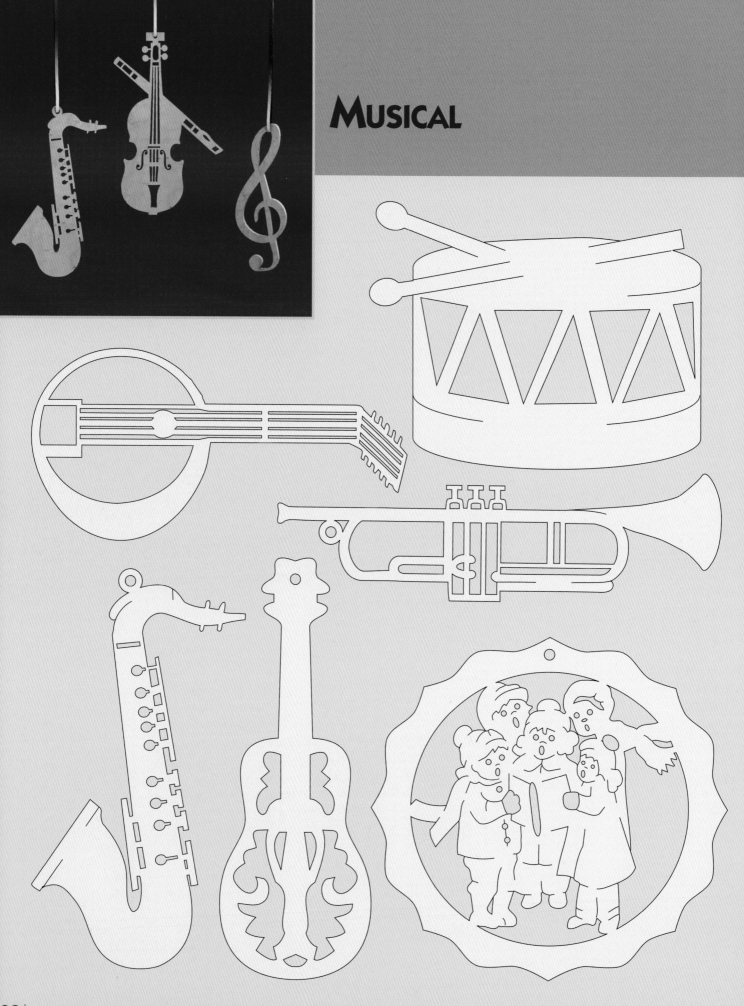

MUSICAL

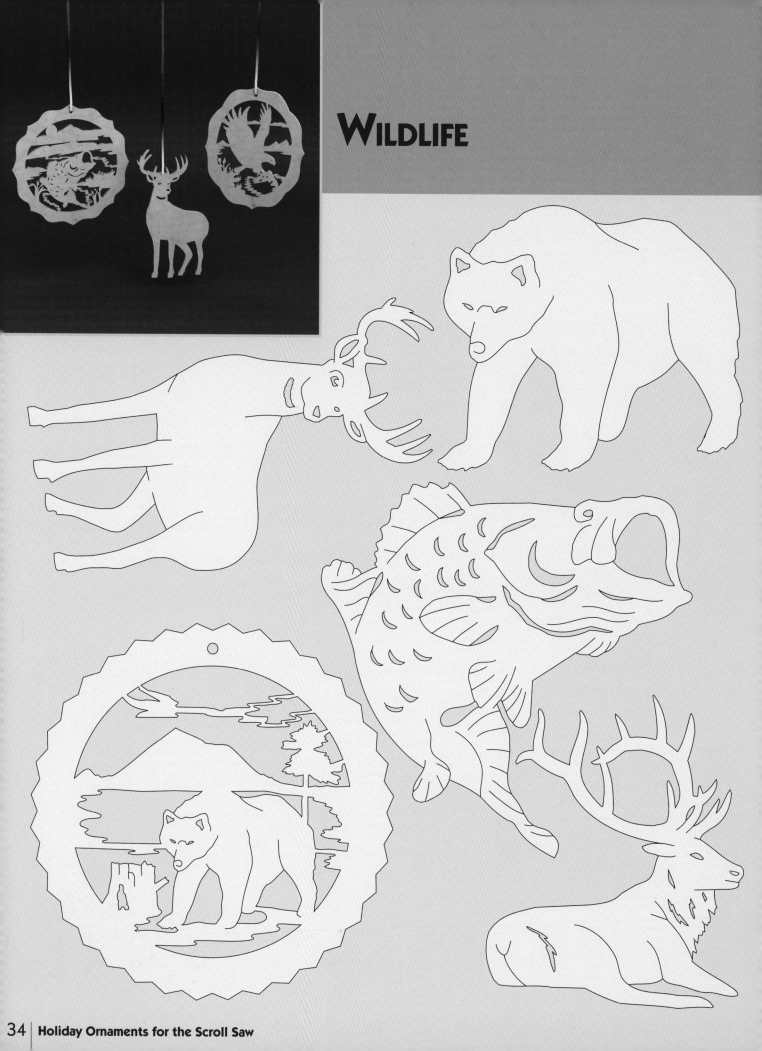

WILDLIFE

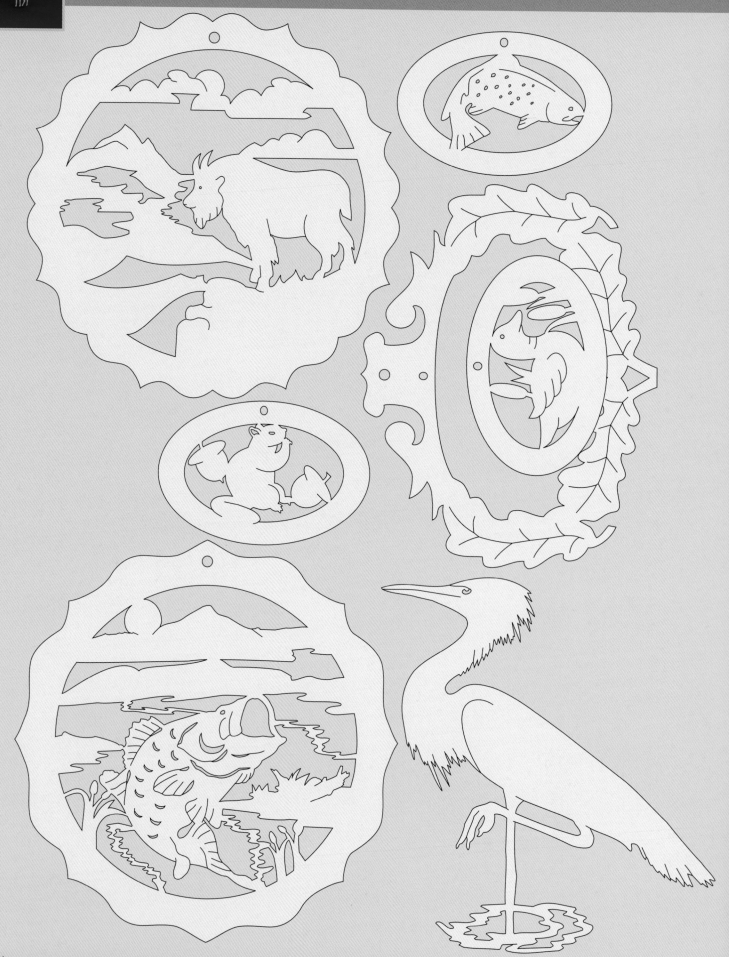

CHILDREN

B
fits here

A
Stock: 1/8"

B
Stock: 1/8"

A
fits here

B
fits here

B
Stock: 1/8"

A
Stock: 1/8"

A
fits here

Dashed line indicates placement of brick wall behind Humpty Dumpty. Attach with glue or silicone.

Attach pieces
with glue or
silicone.

Cut frame for each pair of animals.

Optional: Cut frames for animals. Attach animals to frames with glue or silicone. For a varied effect, 2 of an animal can be cut and attached to the frame in the same or in opposite directions.

Snowflakes and Icicles

Bore 1 3/8" hole
for picture frame

Bore 1 3/8" hole for picture frame

A
Stock: 1/8"

B
fits here

A
fits here

B
Stock: 1/8"

C
fits here

C
fits here

C
Stock: 1/8",
cut 2

B
fits here

VEHICLES

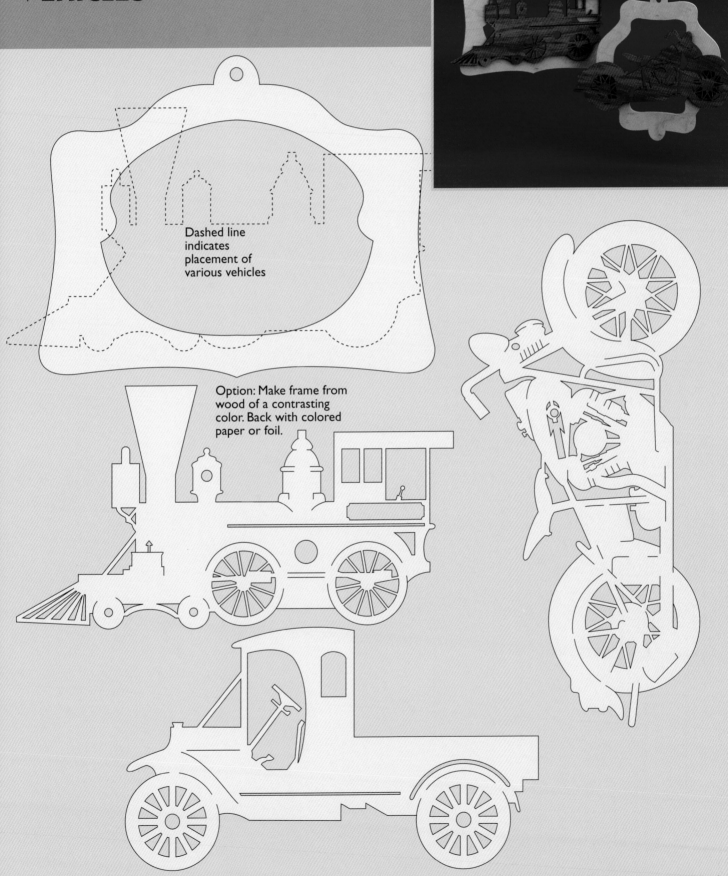

Dashed line indicates placement of various vehicles

Option: Make frame from wood of a contrasting color. Back with colored paper or foil.

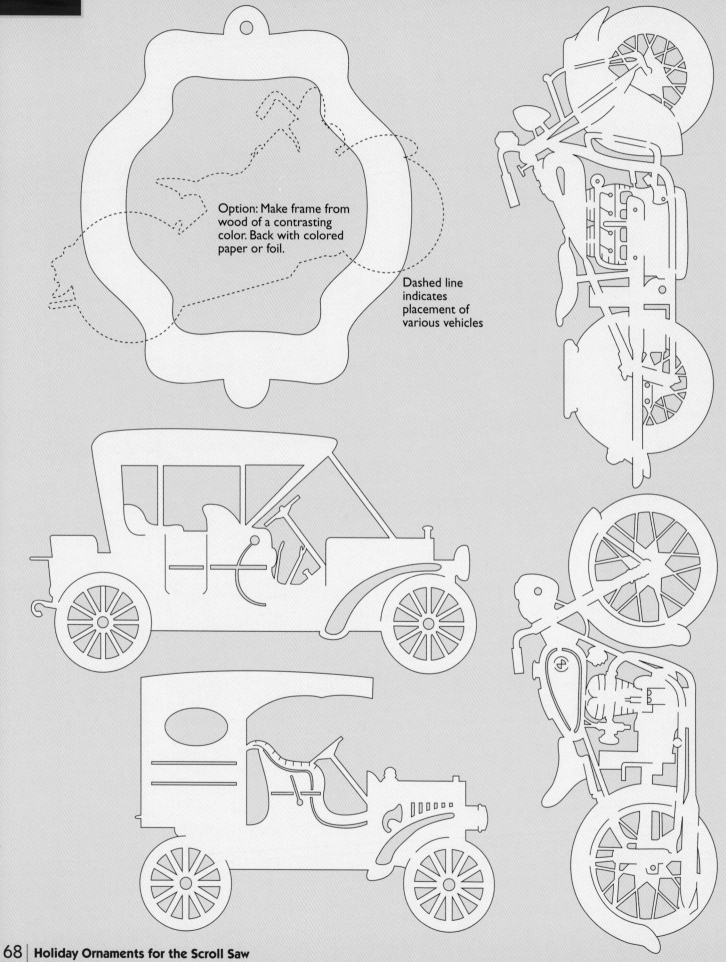

Option: Make frame from wood of a contrasting color. Back with colored paper or foil.

Dashed line indicates placement of various vehicles

RELIGIOUS

VICTORIAN

Stock: 1/8"
Slide the 2 halves
together and
secure with glue.

Bore 1 3/8" hole
for picture frame

Stock: 1/8"

Stock: 1/8"

A fits here

B

B

A fits here

Stock: 1/8"
Attach 2 or 3
hearts together
with glue. Drill hole
in top heart only.

A

A
fits here

B

B
fits here

Stock: 1/8"

Stock: 1/8"

A fits here

A

B
fits here

Stock: 1/8"

Stock: 1/8"

Bore 1 3/8" hole
for picture frame

Bore 1 3/8" hole
for picture frame

WREATHS

Bore 1 3/8" hole
for picture frame

Bore 1 3/8" hole
for picture frame

Bore 1 3/8" hole
for picture frame

Bore 1 3/8" hole
for picture frame

Bore 1 3/8" hole
for picture frame

Bore 1 3/8" hole
for picture frame

Bore 1 3/8" hole
for picture frame

Bore 1 3/8" hole
for picture frame

Bore 1 3/8" hole
for picture frame

Dashed line indicates placement of text.

Choose text and attach to wreath of your choice with glue or silicone.

Love

Silent Night

Merry Christmas

Noel

Dashed line indicates placement of text.

JESUS

Cut out desired letters for banner words and adjust size if needed. Attach with glue or silicone.

HARK

HO HO HO

1 2

Cut out desired letters or numbers for Santa to hold and attach with glue or silicone.

Space letters at bottom of church, drill holes and attach letters with floral wire.

Space letters at bottom of ornament, drill holes and attach letters with floral wire or ribbon. Reduce or enlarge letters and/or numbers as desired.

Space letters at bottom of ornament, drill holes and attach letters with floral wire or ribbon. Reduce or enlarge letters and/or numbers as desired.

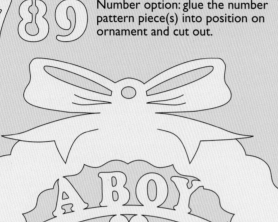

Number option: glue the number pattern piece(s) into position on ornament and cut out.

Glue the overlay numbers or letters in place with glue or silicone.

Dashed line indicates placement of banners.

Dashed lines indicate placement of number overlays.

Classics

Bore 1 3/8" hole
for picture frame

Bore 1 3/8" hole
for picture frame

Bore 1 3/8" hole
for picture frame

Bore 1 3/8" hole
for picture frame

Bore 1 3/8" hole
for picture frame